One person who had entered the Run but was not listed was the Honourable C. S. Rolls (later the Rolls of Rolls-Royce). He had recently purchased an 1896 Peugeot. His non-arrival, according to 'The Automotor and Horseless Vehicle Journal', was due to 'an inadvertence soon after leaving Cambridge'. In this posed picture C. S. Rolls is preceded by a man walking in front. The red flag has been painted in afterwards.

THE BRIGHTON RUN

Lord Montagu of Beaulieu

Shire Publications Ltd

CONTENTS

Printed in Great Britain by C. I. Thomas & Sons (Haverfordwest) Ltd, Press Buildings, Merlins Bridge, Haverfordwest, Dyfed SA61 1XF.

British Library Cataloguing in Publication Data: Montagu of Beaulieu, Edward Douglas-Scott Montagu, Baron. The Brighton Run. 1. South-east England. Cars. Rallies. RAC London-Brighton Run. Cars, history. I. Title. 796.72. ISBN 0-7478-0099-5.

Editorial Consultant: Michael E. Ware, Curator of the National Motor Museum, Beaulieu.

ACKNOWLEDGEMENTS
I would like to thank Michael Ware for his research in connection with this book; the history of the Run has always fascinated him. We have been greatly helped by John Willrich, Lynda Springate and Peter Brockes from the Beaulieu staff as well as by many members of the Veteran Car Club, particularly the late Bernard Garrett, Malcolm Jeal, John Mitchell and Eric Sharman. I am grateful to Nick Georgano for reading the manuscript and making many most helpful comments. Michèle Fiddy typed and re-typed the manuscript. All the photographs are from the National Motor Museum at Beaulieu, with the exception of the cover picture, which is by Michael Bass, and that on page 14 (left), which was kindly supplied by Air Marshal Sir Frederick Sowrey.

Cover: *On a typical chilly and overcast November morning on the 6th November 1988, A. B. Whitelegge leaves Hyde Park driving his two-seater 1903 Humberette at the start of the Brighton Run. This single-cylinder 5 horsepower car is typical of many of the veterans taking part. It carries a 1904 Hampshire registration number.*

This painting is a reconstruction of an incident involving a steam carriage built by John Penn in 1836 for John Hills. The brakes on the steam carriage failed on River Hill, Sevenoaks, Kent, forcing the London stage-coach to take to the ditch. A steam carriage made by John Penn and Sons of Greenwich was entered for the Emancipation Run of 1896 but did not start.

There are very few, if any, unposed photographs of a locomotive travelling on the highway before the Act of 1878 and showing a man walking 60 yards (55 metres) ahead carrying a red flag. This well known photograph taken in 1869 depicts 'Hero', a Tasker self-propelled traction engine, on its way to Southampton Show from the works at Andover. The man has the flag but for the convenience of the photographer he is shown close up to the engine — not an ideal position for warning oncoming horse-drawn traffic.

THE RED FLAG

The annual London to Brighton Run for veteran cars, held nowadays on the first Sunday in November, commemorates the Emancipation Run of 1896 when over thirty pioneer motorists set off for the Sussex seaside to celebrate 'doing away with the red flag'. That is the popular belief but the origin of the Run is not quite as simple as that.

As long ago as 1801 Richard Trevithick demonstrated the practicability of the steam vehicle and he was followed by such pioneers as W. H. Church, Walter Hancock and Goldsworthy Gurney, who turned their motive power to commercial use by building steam road coaches. Hancock, for example, was claiming speeds of between 15 and 20 mph (24-32 km/h) and in the months between August and November 1834 carried over four hundred passengers without accident between the City and Paddington in London.

Most of Britain's main roads were owned by turnpike trusts and they exercised their dislike of the heavy steam vehicle by charging excessive tolls, and steam road coaches soon disappeared. By 1840 there were no steam coaches running a regular service anywhere in Britain. Next came the self-propelled steam traction engine, a development of the horse-drawn portable steam engine. Most of these engines were designed for agricultural use and needed to travel only relatively short journeys on the public road. Those used later for hauling goods could travel further. The Loco-

3

motive Act in 1861 reduced the tolls but fixed a maximum speed of 10 mph (16 km/h), or 5 mph (8 km/h) in towns. It also required the engine to have a crew of two. This was no disadvantage as they were often designed to have a steersman at the front and a driver on the footplate at the rear.

The so-called Red Flag Act of 1865 was the one that led to problems, Section Three requiring that 'at least three persons shall be employed to drive or conduct such a locomotive . . . one of such persons . . . shall precede such locomotive on foot by not less than sixty yards and shall carry a red flag constantly displayed and shall warn drivers and riders of horses of such locomotives.' This Act reduced the speed limit to 4 mph (6 km/h), or 2 mph (3.2 km/h) in towns. Whilst clauses of this Act might seem to make sense on roads which were dominated by equestrian traffic, the Act made no distinction between heavy and light locomotives. It was this point which stifled the development of the car (a light locomotive) in Great Britain.

Parliament set up a select committee in 1873 to look into the Acts and found that in practice they were not working well. On congested roads, a man walking 60 yards (55 metres) ahead of the locomotive could be lost in the traffic. The flapping red flag was said to frighten the horses. In some cases locomotive owners used a boy as a flagman. In 1878 the Highways and Locomotive Amendment Act tackled some of these problems. This Act stipulated that there still had to be three men with each locomotive and one had to precede it by at least 20 yards (18 metres). No mention was made of his having to carry a red flag. A new element was included, however: it was now necessary to have a £10 licence for each county that the locomotive passed through and some counties stipulated the hours in which the locomotive could travel.

The idea of a man preceding a noisy smoky locomotive carrying a warning flag must have seemed sensible to those who were responsible for horse-drawn traffic. So it is very possible that many of those walking the statutory 20 yards ahead would sensibly have still carried the red flag. All motorists would have

been aware of the law and its anomalies and most would have carried a red flag somewhere in their car. Mrs Koosens, in her diary in December 1895, wrote: 'police called at 1.30, took our names [her husband was the driver], re driving through Fareham without a red flag ahead'. They were later fined one shilling and costs of 15s 7d for using a locomotive (a Lutzmann car) without causing a person on foot to precede it by at least 20 yards. In the summons there was no mention of the red flag — only the motorist's diary mentioned that: presumably the Koosens did not have the man 'walking in front'. The *Hampshire Chronicle*, reporting on the case, claimed that Mr Koosens was fined for 'using an auto car without having a signalman twenty yards in front'. Perhaps this is a clue. If one is supposed to be a signalman why not carry a recognisable signal? In February 1896 T. R. B. Elliot of Berwick-on-Tweed was fined for 'using a horseless carriage without having a man on foot preceding it'. There is no mention of a red flag. In the early summonses that I have been able to trace the offence in each case was that of not having a person on foot 20 yards ahead and/or having no locomotive licence, or for operating a locomotive outside the prescribed hours. There is no mention of the red flag as it was not a requirement by law.

In 1895 the Locomotives on the Highway Act was first introduced to Parliament with the full backing of the Liberal Government, led by the Earl of Rosebery. Unfortunately the government fell before it became law, so it was reintroduced next year by Lord Harris in the House of Lords and by the Chairman of the Local Government Board, Henry Chaplin, in the Commons. The Bill did away with the need for three people to be in attendance and for a man to walk in front. It raised the speed limit to 14 mph (22 km/h). Most local government boards had the power to reduce it to 12 mph (19 km/h). There was now no need for self-propelled vehicles under 2 tons to have a licence. All this was celebrated by the Emancipation Run in November 1896. However, the myth of the red flag lingers on.

4

Left: The programme for the Emancipation Run is now a collector's item. According to 'The Automotor and Horseless Vehicle Journal': 'The issue was perhaps one of the largest ever made by a vehicular or trade journal: it was exhausted in the London streets in less than one hour . . . 25,000 could have been absorbed in the Metropolis alone.'

Right: These sketches from an unknown newspaper show the Panhard Parcels Van and the Cannstatt Daimler 'Present Times' battling through the crowds with the Lawson pilot car at the front. The bottom picture depicts the moments just before the start; the third car on the line and possibly the fourth are Léon Bollées. The inset is almost certainly one of the De Dion Bouton tricycles.

THE EMANCIPATION RUN

Great Britain lagged a long way behind the Continent when it came to building the horseless carriage. In Germany Benz had made his first car in 1886, as did Daimler. In France Panhard and Levassor, Peugeot and De Dion Bouton had cars running in the early 1890s. Britain's apparent lethargy was due in part to the restrictive laws described in the last chapter. Those pioneers who did experiment, such as Santler, Bremer, Knight and Lanchester, all had cars running by 1896. The first importations from the Continent came in 1895. I estimate that there were no more than 75 cars in Britain when the Motor Car Club announced that it was going to organise a motor tour to Brighton on the day that

the Act was repealed, 14th November 1896. Motor cars were in their infancy; *The Autocar* in its 'red letter day issue' (they actually printed it in red) could raise only eighteen firms to advertise in its columns, and of these only nine could be said to be manufacturers or people intending to manufacture.

Harry J. Lawson tried to dominate the early days of the British industry. Lawson, who had become rich through his bicycle and tyre companies, founded the British Motor Syndicate with Charles McRobie Turrell in 1895. He bought up the patent rights for Great Britain for Daimler, De Dion Bouton and Léon Bollée, and he also obtained some rather dubious patents from E. J. Pennington of

Chicago. He founded The Great Horse-less Carriage Company in 1896, which was to be the manufacturing company. Lawson was the founder and President of the Motor Car Club, he led the Emancipation event in the pilot car, and his company entered a number of vehicles for promotional purposes. These facts show that the organisation of this first run was not without bias, and this was to be an important factor as events turned out.

Why the Motor Car Club decided to go from London to Brighton is not recorded; certainly they wanted to celebrate the motor car's new-found freedom with more than just a procession through London. From Regency times onwards young bloods had ridden horses

Right: *Seen here taking part in the Lord Mayor's Show in London on the Monday preceding the Emancipation Run in 1896 is the Cannstatt Daimler 'Present Times'. Some idea of the crowds which turned out to public events can be gauged from this photograph. Harry J. Lawson in his speech at Brighton said that the crowds at the Emancipation Run were larger than those for the Lord Mayor's Show.*

A posed picture most probably taken in London a day or two before the Run. This is one of the electric vehicles which were always rumoured to have completed the journey by train. Walter Bersey confirmed the truth of the rumour at the Veteran Car Club dinner in 1935. The electric carriage in those times, as today, was hampered by the lack of accumulator power, so inhibiting its range.

6

Harrods were one of the first London stores to use the horseless carriage. They entered their Daimler, called an omnibus in the programme, and it arrived safely at Brighton.

in relays from London to Brighton and in February 1869 the first run took place on the Brighton Road for boneshaker bicycles, since when it had been used by many cycling clubs. Lawson and many others were ex-cyclists. It is unclear when they first decided on holding the Emancipation Run, but it must have been planned well in advance because it attracted two entries from America (the Duryea brothers) and some well known names from the Continent.

The official programme, published by *The Automotor and Horseless Vehicle Journal (AMJ)*, makes interesting reading as it includes the instructions to the drivers, who had to 'remember that motor cars are on their trial in England and that any rashness or carelessness might injure the industry in this country . . . Special caps and armlets can be provided for members . . .' Oil and petrol were available at Reigate whilst many hostelries were listed as being able to supply water. In view of what happened later, the details of the arrival at Brighton are pertinent: 'Preston Park . . . it is requested that cars should stop to en-

able as many as possible to enter Brighton together . . . the pilot car will head the procession into Brighton.' It concludes with a footnote: 'The British Motor Syndicate [Lawson] who are the owners of several practical motor car patents have kindly consented to waive all rights so as to enable possibly infringing motor cars to take part in the Run.'

Some 58 cars were entered for the event, though only 33 turned up for the start. The pilot car, number 1, was a twin-cylinder Panhard and Levassor which had been successful in the famous Paris to Bordeaux race of 1895. Harry Lawson travelled in this car. From here on the numbering printed in *The Autocar* report of the event and the numbering in the official programme published by *The AMJ* differ. This account uses the version from *The Autocar*. Car number 2 was the Cannstatt Daimler, the first car ever to take part in the Lord Mayor's Show. Car 3 was the Panhard Levassor (with Daimler engine) which won the Paris-Marseilles race in 1896. Car number 12 was a Daimler Wagonette which had finished second in the same race. Car number 4 was a Daimler dog cart belonging to and driven by the Honourable Evelyn Ellis, the man who had previously imported what was probably the first ever car brought into Britain, a Panhard Levassor. There were three three-wheeled Bollées from France, driven by Léon and Camille Bollée and the motoring historian H. O. Duncan. From America came the Duryea brothers with two of their cars — they built a run of thirteen identical cars in 1896, thus starting the American automobile industry. These cars were fast for their day, with a top speed of 20 mph (32 km/h). Duryea had an agent in Britain and five cars had been crated and shipped before the Run. Two were unpacked and entered; the remainder awaited buyers after their anticipated success in the event. Arnold's of East Peckham, who had the British Benz agency along with Henry Hewetson, entered three cars and a van, the latter lettered out for Sunlight Soap. One of these cars still survives, now again in Arnold family ownership and on display at the National Motor Museum.

Most of the cars entered were powered by the internal combustion engine. There were, however, two steamers and seven electric vehicles, three by Bersey and four made by Britannia. E. J. Pennington was gaining a reputation for exaggerated claims in respect of the motor vehicles he had designed, and whilst it is uncertain how many Penningtons started it is recorded that one finished despite suffering a 'blowout'.

The Motor Car Club described the purpose of the event as follows: 'This the first tour of motor cars in England has been arranged to afford local authorities and the public a demonstration of the capabilities of every existing kind of motor vehicle under ordinary circumstances of road traffic.' Historians have tended to brand the organisation of the Emancipation Run as chaotic, and parts of it certainly were. Probably too little thought was given to the Run itself; the possibility of crowds, bad weather, breakdown of the pilot car et cetera did not seem to have been allowed for. It would appear, however, that the organisation of the meals, the hotels, the conveyance of luggage to Brighton and a train for the Press was extremely well done. The Club had tried to arrange a trial run over the route on 24th October but this had to be cancelled because of opposition from Surrey County Council.

Some problems were caused by the Run taking place on the first day on which the new Act came into force. H. O. Duncan, writing in *The World on Wheels*, claims that the three Bollée cars from France were not allowed to run on the roads in London two days before. They had to be towed by horse from

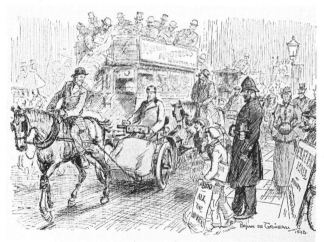

A drawing by Bryan de Grineau of the three Bollées being moved from Victoria station two days before the Act came into force. The police forbade them to run, so they were towed by horse. Though dated 1896, this illustration is thought to have been undertaken in the 1930s when de Grineau was on the staff of 'The Motor'.

The start of the Emancipation Run at the Hotel Metropole, London, with Harry Lawson leading the way in his Phaeton and wearing the uniform which the Motor Car Club had adopted, namely a serge coat with gilt buttons, a peak cap and an armlet on which is embroidered 'the device emblematic of its purpose' ('The Times').

Victoria station to their headquarters, during which the tow-rope broke at least once: 'I felt the full force of the scathing humour of the London street urchin and cabbie.' Presumably they could have run if licensed and preceded by a man walking in front. It was probably the lack of a licence that caused the problems. *The News of the World* reported that 'as soon as the hour of midnight struck not a few enterprising owners had their vehicles upon the streets, and in the small hours of the morning a few cars made trial runs'.

The start of the Run was at the Metropole Hotel in Northumberland Avenue. A grand breakfast was laid on for members of the Motor Car Club, the competitors, their friends and the press. During this meal Lord Winchilsea reminded competitors that motor cars were on trial and that as many of them had not had much time to practise they had to be especially careful. Finally, he dramatically tore up a red flag. Outside great crowds thronged the roads. Throughout

the event the crowds appear to have been enormous. Not all the cars could reach the start, the Arnold contingent, for example, starting two hours late as they could not get through the throng. Pennington had been giving rides and could not get back to the start in time, so he joined the route further down. At 10.30 the first cars left, led by Harry Lawson. This account from *The Daily Graphic* describes many of the problems: 'The roads were filthy and the movement of the crowd formed a constant embarrassment. For the first three or four miles it was seldom possible to get a clear run of more than a hundred yards without stoppage and for the greater part of this first stage only walking pace was possible. This bad beginning for which only the police and the public were responsible was the direct cause of several of the failures later on in the day. It must be explained that when an oil motor is momentarily stopped or checked the machinery goes on working as vigorously as ever and the energy which should have

'We found Reigate in a state of uproar, thousands of people with just a narrow lane through the midst of them down which a single lane of traffic felt its way with difficulty' ('The Autocar').

propelled the vehicle forward only created extra vibration and extra heat. Thus as a consequence of their slow progress from Whitehall to Brixton many of the motors got overheated and worked badly for the rest of the journey.'

The impression that comes through from all the press reports is of huge

Above: *This is the Panhard Levassor which won the Paris to Marseilles race in 1896. It is seen here entering Reigate preceded by a man on foot to clear away the crowds. It was driven by Mr Mayade, who was works manager for Panhard Levassor. He was later the first person ever to be killed in a motor-racing accident.*

Below: *Crowds lined the streets in Reigate. Cyclists are much in evidence, some following the competitors, whilst others have ridden into town to see the spectacle.*

crowds, very muddy roads and poor weather, for it rained most of the day. Then there were the cyclists who followed the Run, often clinging on to the cars themselves. *The Morning Post* thought they must have numbered over a thousand. According to the regulations cars were supposed to stop at the White Hart Hotel in Reigate for lunch. Most cars did but those that did not included at least one of the Bollées. There were a number of minor accidents, the most serious being when a little girl named Mary Dyer, the daughter of a publican, darted out into the road in front of one of the Duryeas and was knocked over; as she lay in the road a cyclist riding behind fell over her. Later the driver of the Duryea was exonerated of all blame. It had been hoped that the cars would go in procession into Brighton and so arrive in some form of order to be presented to the Mayor in Preston Park. But, according to the obviously very wet reporter from *The Brighton Herald*, 'instead of which they struggled in one at a time with long intervals in between and darkness fell before half a dozen of the conveyances had reached their destination'. There was more than a little doubt as to which car was first to get to Brighton. As it was not supposed to be a race this did not matter much except for the fact that many commercial interests were involved.

Harry Lawson issued a statement that evening: 'the following cars duly arrived at Brighton. First at 2.33 a Bollée Voiturette and at 2.47 another Bollée car. Neither of these followed the instruction to wait at Reigate . . . our own cars endeavoured to keep to the original programme, the pilot car and three British Motor Syndicate cars were all four in their proper places at Preston Park, Brighton at 4.30 where they were received by the Mayor of Brighton. An American car followed immediately . . . the committee decided to award gold medals to the first eight motors which arrived in good time. The fact that twenty motors out of the twenty-two which left Brixton arrived at Brighton during the evening without accidents exceeded the committee's most sanguine expectations.' (A figure of 22 leaving Brixton does not tie up with the report in

This is how the artist from 'The Daily Graphic' saw the Run. Whilst the view of the vehicles coming into Reigate will now be familiar, there appear to be a few other illustrations of the cars entering Preston Park for the official finish. The rainy conditions are well illustrated.

Whatever the officials may say, the artist from 'The Penny Illustrated Paper' thought the Duryea was the first car at Reigate. Here they stopped for lunch at the White Hart Hotel. The Bollée cars went straight on without a lunch stop. Even the paper termed it a race!

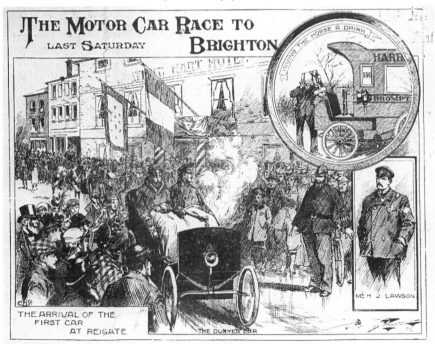

Few photographs of the cars on the move outside the towns exist. This is one of a series given to the National Motor Museum. It shows the 4 horsepower Panhard Levassor driven by Mr Thompson-Smith and accompanied by a few of the hundreds of cyclists who were on the road that day.

The Autocar.)

Later George Thrupp, passenger on the leading Duryea, swore an affidavit which stated that they left London at 10.40 and arrived at the White Hart Hotel, Reigate, at 12.40, where they stopped for lunch, leaving at 1.45, and arrived at the Hotel Metropole, Brighton at 3.45, and it finishes by categorically stating: 'we were the first motor carriage to arrive at Reigate, our first stopping place, and also at Brighton.' H. O. Duncan, later writing in *The World on Wheels,* made the following comment: 'it was quite natural for Lawson and his Syndicate not to take any notice of the presence in the Brighton Run of the Duryea cars. Not having purchased any

patents covering this car he was not interested in the performance.' As to which car was first at Brighton, I would like to believe the sworn affidavit from the Duryea team. However, if the Bollée failed to stop for lunch at Reigate, they must have been well down the road when the Duryeas left the White Hart after their stop. There is no record that the Bollées were overtaken, so the Bollées must have 'won the race'. I can only assume that George Thrupp dismissed the Bollées as not being a true 'motor carriage' as they had three wheels, whereas the Duryea had four.

The statistics for the event published in *The Autocar* claim that 58 competitors entered, 54 were printed in the pro-

'At Albourne seven miles from Brighton a humorous blacksmith had put a notice "Motor cars stop here for repairs"! It proved prophetic as a car actually broke down near there and was detained for about an hour whilst the defect was being repaired' ('News of the World'). This illustration depicting the scene appeared in 'The Motor' in their issue celebrating the fortieth anniversary of the Run in 1936.

Saturday, November 14th, 1896.

MENU

THE MOTOR CAR CLUB

DINNER

IN CELEBRATION OF THE PASSING OF THE

LOCOMOTIVES ON HIGHWAYS ACT, 189?

THE "MAGNA CHARTA" OF MOTOR CARS,

FIRST MOTOR CAR TOUR LONDON TO BRIGHTO?

BY INVITATION OF MR. HARRY J. LAWSON,

PRESIDENT OF THE MOTOR CAR CLUB,

Left: It was dark by the time the first of the 'official procession' arrived at the Hotel Metropole and Lawson had lit the sidelamps on the pilot car. It was a very wet evening but, even so, great crowds stayed to see the cars in. (Photograph kindly supplied by Air Marshal Sir Frederick Sowrey.)

Right: The cover of the menu for the dinner after the Emancipation Run. After dinner there were many speeches. Harry Lawson made the audience laugh with one reference to speed: 'the law forbade him to travel at more than 12 mph though trotting horses, cyclists and butcher's boys might travel at any rate they liked.' He went on to say that some cyclists and horses overtook his car during the Run.

gramme and 33 started. Some never intended to go the whole route but 28 passed through Streatham, 22 through Reigate, and fifteen were at Brighton by 6.30. Thirteen were declared official finishers. Twenty were in the garage after dinner that night. All eleven cars of the Great Horseless Carriage Company finished. The list of finishers published in *The Autocar* differs from that in *The AMJ*. *The Autocar* list included the Duryea as being third, but *AMJ* leaves it out altogether and includes two electric cars amongst the finishers. However, as *The Autocar* said: 'The electric cars whose accumulators did not carry sufficient power to take them through the journey had not started with any intention of going further than Brixton . . . one by one they found their way to the railway station and made their way to Brighton by that means.'

On the Sunday thousands of Brightonians lined the sea-front to watch the cars as they gave demonstration runs. This was an informal display. Lawson would not bring his cars out 'but the Duryea was let loose, rushed about in an alarmingly dangerous manner, at almost twice the maximum speed allowed by law and it was a wonder that no accidents resulted'. By Monday morning the cars had been cleaned and made to look smart. They formed up outside the Hotel Metropole, where a whole series of photographs was taken. Later they paraded in orderly fashion and according to *The Brighton Gazette and Sussex Telegraph*: 'the parade was witnessed by another large concourse of people who never tired of discussing the merits and appearances of the vehicles. It seemed a general consensus of opinion that the height of beauty had certainly not been attained in the matter of construction though there were one or two which called for admiration.'

The party broke up on Tuesday and according to *The Autocar* 'ten cars set out from the Hotel Metropole, Brighton at 10.15 on Tuesday morning and at 2.30 on the same afternoon the first car, driven by Mr M. Mayade, carrying M. Harrington Moore, Secretary of the Motor Car Club, arrived at the Hotel Metropole [London] . . . the return journey was completed in a little over 3½ hours actual running time . . .' There are rumours that two of them were French racing cars and were 'seen going at a rate of about 30 mph'.

The running time of 3½ hours makes an interesting comparison with the fastest road coach time ever recorded between London and Brighton of 3 hours 36 minutes, and this included many changes of horses.

The Motor Car Club held a re-enactment of the Emancipation Run each year until 1902. They did not go to Brighton as they were looking for venues that would enable them to go there and back in a day. Sheen House, Richmond, and Oxford were two of the destinations. Another big event was planned for the tenth anniversary in 1906 but this ended up as a luncheon.

Left: The Bollée was later marketed in Great Britain as the Coventry Motette. In this advertisement the British Motor Syndicate is claiming it won the London to Brighton Race. At the time of the event itself Harry Lawson and others were at pains to point out that it was not a race!

Right: This 4 horsepower Panhard van was driven on the Run by Charles E. Rush. He wrote after the event: 'my drive to Brighton was not altogether the greatest success . . . my chief trouble was the pump and water cooling which together with a lack of petrol owing to my having given some away delayed my arrival until long after the memorable dinner had been eaten and digested . . . the run back was made under most successful conditions.'

Above left: *The Motor Car Club awarded medals to eight finishers for the 1896 event. They had to admit the success of the Duryea and awarded it a medal, now in the Smithsonian Institution in Washington.*

Above right: *The Brighton and Sussex Goldsmiths Association had three medals engraved to commemorate the Emancipation Run. At the dinner at the Hotel Metropole the Mayor of Brighton, Alderman J. G. Blaker, presented them to H. J. Lawson as Chairman of the Motor Car Club, to Mr Harrington-Moore and to C. M. R. Turrell. One of these medals is now owned by Sir Len Southward in New Zealand.*

Below: *YU 1974 was the first Cadillac to be imported into Europe. That was in 1903, the year of its manufacture. This photograph shows it 25 years later, taking part in the second re-enactment. The car was owned and entered by Fred Bennett of St John's Wood. The car is still owned by the original family and is on loan to the museum at Beaulieu.*

At this spot the Brighton Run looks very rural; this is the 1933 Run. The car is Ken Harlow's 1901 MMC. MMC stands for Motor Manufacturing Company, whose origins were in those of Harry Lawson's Great Horseless Carriage Company of Coventry.

THE OLD CROCKS RACE

It was Robert de Baire, motoring editor of *The Daily Sketch*, who in 1927 had the idea of undertaking a re-enactment of the 1896 Run. He enlisted the co-sponsorship of *The Sunday Graphic* and the two newspapers ran the event in 1927. The following year they had help from *The Autocar*, but for 1929 it was just the two papers again. From 1930 to the present day the event has been professionally organised by the Royal Automobile Club (RAC). For 1927 no less than 51 pre-1906 cars (21 years old or over) entered. In the early years the age of eligibility changed. In 1928 the cars had to be 25 years old on 18th November, so that 1903 was the most recent date, whilst in 1929 (when the event was held on 20th October instead of the usual November date) they still had to be 25 years old (October 1904). The RAC established a firm rule in 1930, when they stipulated a latest date of 31st December 1904, which is still adhered to today. It was not until 1934 that the Veteran Car Club started issuing certificates of eligibility. Until then there had been much argument about the dates of various cars. Apparently the 1909 Humber in my own collection once took part in those early years!

Modern-day veteran-car owners shudder at the title 'Old Crocks Race', which they have been trying to live down for years, but that was how the event was first described not only in the daily newspapers but in *The Autocar* as well.

For 1927 the Run started on the Victoria Embankment and finished at Patcham in Brighton. Once assembled at the finish, the cars paraded to the Madeira Drive. From 1928 onwards the cars were assembled at a chosen garage in London and then went in order to a start on Westminster Bridge. In 1930 the finish was changed to the Aquarium Garage in Brighton. The start at the City of London Garage from 1934 was criticised as the cars had to wend their way through crowded streets on the Saturday to get

there. On Sunday, when all the cars started up, fumes caused problems: 'one driver fainted and many suffered headaches for days after the Run.' In 1936, the fortieth anniversary year, the Run started from the Magazine, Hyde Park, and the finish was alongside the sea on the Madeira Drive. This was thought to be rather a tame ending and so in 1938 all those cars which were at the finish by three o'clock paraded along the front to

Left: *C. H. Perrin and his crew seem very pleased to have made it to Madeira Drive in 1936. The car is a Cannstatt Daimler similar in many ways to 'Present Times', which was on the Emancipation Run. This car was later re-dated by the Veteran Car Club to 1898. It was owned for some years by G. James Allday, a past President of the Veteran Car Club, before passing to the National Motor Museum Trust at Beaulieu.*

Below: *Lanchester had a car running in Great Britain a year before the Emancipation Run. It was reputed to have been in pieces in November 1896 and so could not take part. This 1901 Lanchester is competing in the 1928 event, driven by Lord Ridley from Northumberland. The car is crossing Westminster Bridge with the Houses of Parliament and Big Ben in the background.*

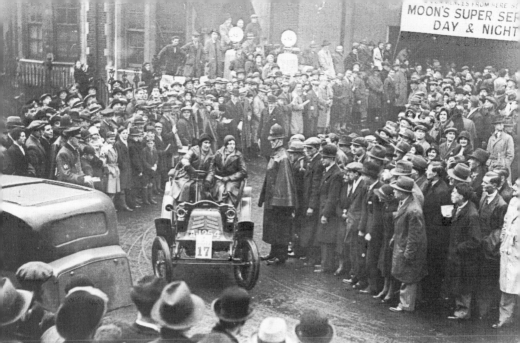

Above: Crowds gather on a grey morning to watch the cars leave Moon's Garage at the start of the 1932 event. Mrs E. L. Wood is setting off with her 1900 (then dated 1899) Pieper, a small car from Belgium. The firm gave up car manufacturing in 1903. Note the RAC patrolman on the left selling programmes, something they still do today on the Run.

Left: In 1930 the RAC issued a Finisher's Certificate, the text of which still mentioned the red flag. The centre part of the certificate was a Gordon Crosby cartoon, which also adorned the cover of the programme for the Run from 1928 until 1956, though it was slightly altered in later years. The cartoonist pokes fun at the red flag man but he depicts a speeding car which looks more like 1903 than 1896!

ROYAL AUTOMOBILE CLUB

LONDON TO BRIGHTON

COMMEMORATION RUN

20th November, 1932.

THIS IS TO CERTIFY THAT

Mr C S Burney

Driving   *Benz.*

Completed the journey from London to Brighton on the occasion of the R.A.C. Commemoration Day Run for Early Cars in *4¼d. 1min 30sec*, at an average speed of *13.98 m p.h.*

The Run was held to celebrate the *36th* Anniversary of Emancipation Day, when the Act of 1896 came into force first permitting motor cars to run upon the highway without being preceded by a man carrying a red flag.

Royal Automobile Club,
Pall Mall, London, S.W.

Regency Square and back, so giving the crowds another opportunity to see the cars. This parade continued until 1962.

The event was never a race, despite the earlier publicity. For one year only, 1929, there were money prizes of £100, £50 and £25. By 1930 the RAC was offering a certificate of finishing. For 1931 there was a modern pilot car which travelled to Brighton at 30 mph (48 km/h), and competitors were told: 'the pilot car will lead to prevent competitors from attempting to race.' How Lawson would have loved this! In the same year a team prize was awarded. In 1934 all those that arrived at Brighton by the finishing time got a medal, a copy of the one presented

19

Above: *Many famous racing drivers such as B. Bira, George Easton, Kay Don and Dick Seaman drove cars in the Run in the 1930s. In 1932 Malcolm Campbell took this 1904 Sunbeam to Brighton and is seen here leaving the start at Moon's Super Service Garage. Possibly this was his slowest drive of the year — the fastest being his 253.97 mph (409 km/h) average to take the world land speed record in the Napier Campbell (Bluebird).*

Below left: *Doug Copley was one of the characters of the early re-runs. Here he is passing through Reigate in his 1898 Daimler on the 1928 Run. In the programme he challenges other cars of the same age to a 200 mile (320 km) race. Doug always drove his car from Birmingham to the start of the Run and back to the Midlands again afterwards, unlike others who used lorries or even took their cars on the train.*

Below right: *The first re-enactment of the Run under sponsorship of 'The Daily Sketch' and 'The Sunday Graphic' in 1927. Stephen Statham is seen here crossing Westminster Bridge in the 1899 (then dated 1896) Daimler. 51 cars were entered for the event, which caused 'The Autocar' to remark: 'it may come as something of a surprise to most motorists to realise that there are so many as 51 hale and hearty old cars . . . to undertake the Run from London to Brighton.'*

Readers of 'The Autocar' were reminded in the issue of 22nd November 1935 that certain technical features of the veteran car were totally unfamiliar to the 'modern motorist'. (Clockwise, from top left) A contracting brake lined with wood on the Pannard; geared-down steering, one of the features of the Bollée; a De Dion suction-operated inlet valve; a 1902 Napier dashboard full of drip feed lubricators; a Benz belt drive typical of a car of the period; an early inlet system on a Leon Bollée, which has only one jet.

to the Arnold Motor Company at the end of the 1896 event. For 1936 the cars were classified by age and an average speed was set for each group. Exceeding the speed by 10 per cent (later amended to fifteen minutes) meant exclusion from the medals. A secret check 'short of Redhill' took its toll the first year. A lunch stop at Crawley at the Southdown Bus Company depot was also instigated, although by 1938 this had been moved to 'a car park at the rear of the Embassy Picture House'.

With the exception of 1936, entries for the Run increased each year. From 51 in 1927 they had grown to 121 by 1938. There was no Run in 1939 because of the war. In most years the majority of the entries actually started the Run and the maximum number to fail in any one year was as low as twelve. Entry had been free until 1931, when a charge of 5 shillings was made. The RAC undertook to insure the cars on the Run within this fee, which raised the old problem of what a veteran car is worth. The RAC settled it by insuring each car for £100.

In the earlier years fun was poked at the owners, but the term 'old crock' was officially dropped by 1930. There were those who questioned the wisdom of *The Daily Sketch*, who lined the Brighton road in 1928 with placards which read 'Come and laugh at the old crocks'. It must be admitted that in the first years some cars did carry amusing placards such as 'Expiring tonight' or 'Don't shoot the driver, he's doing his best', and in 1930 one car had the passenger playing a tune on a coaching horn as his 'audible warning device'. Racing driver Sammy Davis wrote in *The Autocar* that year that 'such little comic elements as were apparent . . . were quelled quite nicely and firmly'. Fancy dress or even appropriate period costume has always been frowned upon, although the clothes worn by some crews to keep out the cold and the rain are often more than slightly bizarre.

After the Run of 1930 Sammy Davis of *The Autocar*, and Captain John Wylie, both regular competitors, and Jackie Masters, an official, were drinking in the Old Ship Hotel when they had the idea of forming the Veteran Car Club (VCC). It was the impetus given by this club which created the enthusiasm that enabled many old cars to be found again, and so entries for the Run gradually increased. 1931 was the first year of the co-operation between the VCC and the RAC which still exists. By 1932 the VCC were holding a dinner at Brighton after the Run, which also still happens today.

In the light of the hiatus after the Emancipation Run, the speech at the VCC dinner in 1935 by Walter Bersey must have stunned many of the audience. He admitted that his electric car on that first Run went to Brighton by train, 'when it was hidden around the corner to

In the 1928 Run the Sunbeam Motor Car Company entered one of their early models, a 1901 2¾ horsepower Sunbeam Mabley. The De Dion Bouton engine at the front drives the offset rear wheel, whilst the two side wheels are there to give stability. The seating is like a Victorian chaise-longue with the driver at the back peering over the shoulder of the passenger. It is accompanied by two Austin Chummys and a number of motorcycles.

await the other competitors'. He also admitted covering the vehicle with mud to make it look as if it had been on the Brighton road. He remarked that he had difficulty in finding mud of the right colour!

Racing driver Kay Don did not endear himself to the veteran-car world by what he wrote in a column in *The Lincolnshire Echo* in 1937 under the title 'Banish Old Crocks'. He claimed that their poor brakes made them unsafe and that the car he drove, a 1900 De Dion Bouton, 'was ready to slide at the slightest provocation'.

One of the principal hazards was the road surface itself, although it had much improved since 1896. Wooden blocks were, however, very greasy when wet and tram lines were the cause of many a 'dreaded side slip' if you caught them at the wrong angle. If you drove a narrow-tyred car such as a Benz and the wheel dropped into the tram line, some say you had to follow it to the depot. There are a number of reports of greasy road surfaces being especially sanded to help the veterans.

Below left: C. G. Queton in his 1902 Wolseley has time to wave to photographer W. J. Brunell at the top of Pyecombe Hill on the 1928 re-enactment. Pyecombe Hill is the last uphill gradient on the Brighton road. Because of congestion in Brighton the timed finish of the Run in modern times has shifted to the Pylons, a mile or so on from this location.

Below right: 1938 was the last Run held before the war. Hostilities had commenced before the 1939 Run could take place. Stanley Sears in his 1903 Darracq (then dated 1904) is looking very pleased with himself. This car was one of the veterans which was discovered as a result of the Runs to Brighton and the founding of the Veteran Car Club. It came from Bournemouth, where it had been in a shed for 28 years. Stanley Sears was later to become President of the VCC.

Taking part in the 1932 event is C. S. Burney in his 1901 Benz. The programme tantalisingly goes on to say: 'this is a car that was rescued from burial in Plymouth'. The original owner, Dr Rease of Plymouth, who took part in the 1927 re-enactment, threatened in 1930 to bury the car rather than pay rates of 50 shillings on the shed in which the car was kept. He was, however, persuaded by C. S. Burney not to bury the car but to part with it instead.

That excellent journalist and veteran-car enthusiast Sammy Davis said in 1938 that though there had been 121 entries for the Run that year he knew of at least ten eligible cars which were not on the Run. He went on: 'R. O. Shuttleworth actually believes there are about a hundred machines derelict about the country . . . and the number in France might easily run into hundreds because over there they rarely throw anything away.' Little did he know.

This 1902 Renault taking part in the 1928 Run was entered by the well known garage and coachbuilding firm of Vincent's of Reading. It is running on trade plates, something which is not allowed today. The car is passing the White Hart in Reigate, the lunch stop on the original Run of 1896. The AC and the Bullnose Morris are now more than twice as old as the veteran Renault was at the time the picture was taken.

There would appear to be great interest shown in the first Run after the Second World War. Not only are there large crowds on both sides of the road but also plenty of vehicles, including a Jowett Kestrel, a rare sight even for 1946. The veteran is Lieutenant Commander E. P. Shaw's 1904 Minerva.

THE POST-WAR YEARS

The first post-war run, held in 1946, took place during a period of severe petrol rationing but had a record entry of 136. Part of the increase can be attributed to the foresight of the Veteran Car Club in introducing an acquisition scheme in 1942. This was to stop veteran cars going for scrap. If a car was found or one already known about was threatened, the club would step in and buy it and in due course sell it on to a club member. In this

way many cars were saved — some, of course, dated later than 1904.

By now the format of the event was well established — only minor changes followed. The Run was cancelled in 1947 because of the withdrawal of the petrol ration and in 1948 the Crawley stop was done away with. Cars were then divided into classes, each one having its own average speed, with the possible penalty of exclusion if you travelled faster than

Taking part in the 1952 Run is F. Reece driving his Spyker, which was about to be made famous playing the supporting role in the film 'Genevieve'. 'Genevieve' it-self was a Darracq. Both cars were then believed to date from 1904 but both have now been re-dated by the Veteran Car Club as 1905 and are therefore no longer eligible for the Run. It was the popularity of the film 'Genevieve' that helped to launch the old car movement as we know it today.

For some years a compulsory lunch stop was made in Crawley but it was not popular and was done away with after the Second World War. In 1946 competitors used the car park behind the Embassy Cinema in Crawley. It looks a very damp day.

your set speed. In 1952 the date was fixed as the first Sunday in November and it was during this Run that the Rank Film Organisation took a lot of the establishing shots for *Genevieve*. This film consists of an unofficial race back from Brighton the day after the event — shades of 1896! Because of the film the crowds watching the Run were said to have reached two or three million in 1953 and 1954. In 1955 the cars were in groups of about thirty, the groups leaving at five-

The Brighton road tends to get congested. In 1954 W. T. Gross in his 1902 Wolseley (note the VCC official dating plate) wends his way between an Austin Ten, a Ford BB lorry and a National Benzole Morris Commercial petrol tanker.

Above: *Steam and the internal combustion engine on the eightieth anniversary of the Run in 1976. On the right is the 1896 Daimler Wagonette from the Museum of British Road Transport at Coventry. Peter Mitchell in the passenger seat may well look worried as the car was about to make an involuntary stop. Overtaking it is the Locomobile Steamer belonging to Alec Hodsdon. Though bright, it is raining, and the umbrella on the steamer is a nice touch.*

Below left: *Johnny Thomas from South Wales, completely dwarfed by London buses, driving a three-wheel Léon Bollée of 1896. This vehicle is similar to the ones which took part in the Emancipation Run. The date is 1971, a year in which three of these early Bollées were entered. The weather is obviously warm and the sun is shining.*

Below right: *One of the oldest British cars ever to attempt the Run to Brighton was the Bremer, which was given the coveted number one position in 1963. The car was built by F. W. Bremer of Walthamstow. It is thought to have run in 1894 and has been dated to that year. In the early 1960s it was removed from the Walthamstow Museum and restored by Reg Trott. Here a certain amount of outside assistance is required.*

Above left: *Overseas enthusiasts enter the Brighton Run in quite large numbers. Here on the 1973 Run G. R. Howard from the USA safely negotiates the streets on the outskirts of London in the 1904 air-cooled Franklin. The Brighton Run is known worldwide as the premier veteran car event.*

Above right: *Calamity near Croydon Airport. Dr A. T. Robinson loses a wheel on his Phoenix Tricar. The passenger looks remarkably unperturbed while the police prepare to lend a hand. There are relatively few accidents on the Run; the usual problem is veterans nudging modern cars that slow down quickly in front of them.*

Left: *It almost looks as if this Whitney steamer of E. L. Davis is about to be overwhelmed by a London bus as it crosses Westminster Bridge in 1971. Steam cars are always popular with the crowds because of their silent progress and the small cloud of steam behind. The passenger appears to have found something which requires his urgent attention behind the splashboard.*

minute intervals, and the same practice exists today. In 1956, the sixtieth anniversary of the Run, the RAC gave a special plaque to all finishers. The start was moved to the other end of the Serpentine Road though the route still took in Constitution Hill and the Mall to Westminster Bridge. Because of the severe congestion the Run was now causing, the police fixed a limit of 250 cars in 1961. This continued until recently, when four hundred became the upper limit. To gain this higher number, competitors had to agree to tender vehicles and cars towing trailers taking a different route to Brighton, so helping relieve the congestion. Commercial sponsorship came to the Run in 1972, the first sponsor being BL-Unipart, to be followed by Castrol in their 75th year of 1974.

My first Brighton Run was in 1950 when I took as my passenger the model Barbara Goalen. In this picture the faithful 1903 De Dion Bouton is passing through Norbury. The 1947 Hillman Minx behind was my first new car, the number plate AA19 being the first number issued to my father in 1904. My father's second number, AA20, was transferred to the De Dion in 1910.

A PERSONAL VIEW

My first experience of the Run was in 1950 when I took the 1903 De Dion Bouton with top model Barbara Goalen as my passenger. This car had been on the Beaulieu Estate since 1903 (for the 1950 Run it had been wrongly dated as 1900) and came into the family in 1910 in exchange for a bad debt. Since that time it had been used as an estate hack, mainly by the Beaulieu Electric Light Company! This was some years before the Montagu Motor Museum came into being and I had no experience of rebuilding such a car. Unfortunately we broke down with trembler coil trouble some 6 miles (10 km) from the finish. Later it was restored for me by Sir Alex Coryton, who drove it back to Beaulieu from Bristol for the first opening to the public of my home, Palace House, in 1952, where it took the place of honour, together with four other cars, in the

Front Hall, and thus was born the Montagu Motor Museum.

My next Run was 1955 and I have hardly missed one since. I have driven a wide range of cars from the Beaulieu museum, the De Dion being the slowest and the 1903 Gordon Bennett Napier by far the fastest. My passengers have included His Royal Highness Prince Michael of Kent, politicians, racing drivers, Miss World and stars from show business. I have usually managed to get there, although at times I have received much help from the museum's skilled engineers. In 1987 my passenger was the disc jockey Dave Lee Travis, who was doing his Sunday morning BBC radio programme live from the front seat of my father's second car, the 1899 Daimler. We developed a severe overheating problem and Dave was amazed to see and be able to tell the listeners how

Howard Wilson, the museum's Chief Engineer, took off his leather trouser belt and made up a new drive belt for the water pump from it! My most embarrassing experience was in 1988, when taking the then Secretary of State for Transport, the Right Honourable Paul Channon, in the 1903 Napier. We broke down with a burnt-out clutch opposite the Houses of Parliament, only about a mile from the start!

The Run has an atmosphere all of its own. I know of no other old-car event in the world quite like it, and I have been privileged to take part in many. This is backed up by the number of overseas competitors who enter each year and I am sure they would agree with my sentiments. You take part whatever the weather and sometimes it is dreadful. I have known hail, fog or freezing rain, and I have spent many a mile sitting in a puddle of very cold water. Sometimes the sun shines and that is a real bonus.

Rain plays havoc with leather driving belts on the earlier cars and often reduces braking to a 'gentle rubbing noise'. It is the crowds that really make the event. They line the road from start to finish, and they too have to put up with the weather, but they wave, they cheer and every one of them exhorts you to blow your bulb horn! They are marvellous. The main problem is the very heavy traffic on the Brighton road. Modern car drivers do not appreciate the problems associated with driving a veteran. Veterans cannot stop quickly and it is not always possible to give a hand signal — you often need three hands to drive some of them! But then I suppose I have to agree with Sammy Davis writing on the same problem in 1936 who believed that 'they were a legitimate hazard of the competition'.

Veteran cars are not the only preserved vehicles that have events on the Brighton road. In 1930 the Sunbeam

In 1964 I took the racing driver Jim Clark (seen here driving) on the Run in the 1903 60 horsepower Mercedes owned by the Harmsworth family. Within sight of the finish on the Madeira Drive the car stopped and Jim Clark and the passengers had to push it over the line. Jim Clark, who previously had been robbed of the World Championship on the last lap of the Mexico Grand Prix, remarked: 'I'm getting used to last-lap dramas.'

Above: *In 1970 I drove the 1899 Daimler which was my father's second car. My passenger on that occasion was Tony Blackburn. The car has an interesting history in that it was the first British-made car to race on the Continent in 1899, and the first car to drive into the courtyard of the Houses of Parliament; also my father ran it successfully throughout the 1000 Mile Trial of 1900, possibly the second most important early motoring event after the Emancipation Run.*

Right: *On 4th October 1983 Richard Noble broke the land speed record in Thrust 2, at 633.468 mph (1019.44 km/h). A month later he completed the Run safely in my 1903 De Dion Bouton. In this picture I am greeting Richard and his wife Sally at Brighton, with Geoffrey Rose, Chairman of the RAC. Behind to the left is Anthony Marsh, who has commentated at the finish of virtually every Brighton Run since about 1970.*

Motor Cycle Club held their first Pioneer Run for veteran motorcycles, which now starts at Epsom and runs to Brighton each March. The Historic Commercial Vehicle Society, of which I am President, held its first London to Brighton Run for commercial vehicles in 1962 and this takes place on the first Sunday in May each year.

30

FURTHER READING

There are no other books which have been written specifically about the Brighton Run. However, many books have been written over the years which cover the subject of veteran cars, either in general terms or on specific single makes. The following general books have been published in recent years and should still be available from booksellers or public libraries. For anyone contemplating research into any aspect of the veteran car, the Library of the National Motor Museum at Beaulieu is available free of charge. The Library is open seven days a week, but a prior appointment would be helpful.

Bishop, G. *The Age of the Automobile*. Hamlyn, 1977.
Burgess-Wise, D. *The Motor Car — An Illustrated International History*. Orbis, 1977.
Drackett, P., and Georgano, G. N. *The Encyclopedia of the Motor Car*. Octopus, 1979.
Flower, Raymond, and Wynn-Jones, Michael. *One Hundred Years of Motoring*. RAC, 1981.
Georgano, G. N. (editor). *The Complete Encyclopaedia of Motor Cars 1885-1982*. Ebury Press, 1982. Describes every make of veteran car.
Georgano, G. N., and Montagu of Beaulieu, Lord. *Early Days on the Road*. Universe Books, 1976.
Hodges, D., and Burgess-Wise, D. *The Story of the Car*. Hamlyn, 1974.
Montagu of Beaulieu, Lord. *Antique Cars*. Golden Press, 1974.
Montagu of Beaulieu, Lord, and McComb, F. Wilson. *Behind the Wheel*. Paddington Press, 1977.
Nicholson, T. R. *The Birth of the British Motor Car*, volumes 1-3. Macmillan, 1982.
Roberts, Peter. *A Pictorial History of the Automobile*. Grosset and Dunlap, 1977.
Sedgwick, Michael. *Veteran Cars*. Ward Lock, 1980.
Smith, Maurice (editor). *The Car*. St Michael, 1979.
History of the Motor Car. New English Library, 1971.

MAGAZINES
Apart from the magazine of the Veteran Car Club of Great Britain, there is no one publication which deals specifically with veteran cars. The following magazines, however, often carry articles on this subject:

The Automobile: Acorns, Oak Lane, Easterton, Devizes, Wiltshire SN10 4PD.
Motor Sport: Standard House, Bonhill Street, London EC2A 4DA.

MOTOR CLUBS

The Brighton Run is organised each year by the RAC Motor Sports Association Limited. The Secretary of the Meeting, from whom all details can be obtained, is Mrs Susan Winwood, RAC Motor Sports Association Limited, Motor Sports House, Riverside Park, Colnbrook, Slough, Berkshire SL3 0HG. Telephone: 0753 681736.

The only club in Britain which specifically caters for Brighton Run type vehicles is the Veteran Car Club of Great Britain, Jessamine House, 15 High Street, Ashwell, Hertfordshire. Telephone: 046274 2818. There are many single-make clubs which cater for owners of veteran cars of a particular type, and there are many local old car clubs that welcome owners of veteran cars. A list of such clubs can be obtained from the National Motor Museum at Beaulieu.

PLACES TO VISIT

There are many museums in Britain and Ireland which have large collections of cars, but the following are known to have veteran cars and memorabilia and accessories of the period. Intending visitors are advised to find out the opening times before making a special journey.

Birmingham Museum of Science and Industry, Newhall Street, Birmingham, West Midlands B3 1RZ. Telephone: 021-236 1022.

Caister Castle Motor Museum, West Caister, Great Yarmouth, Norfolk NR30 5SN. Telephone: 057284 251.

Cotswold Motor Museum, The Old Mill, Bourton-on-the-Water, Gloucestershire. Telephone: 0451 21255.

Filching Manor Motor Museum, Filching Manor, Wannock, Polegate, East Sussex BN26 5QA. Telephone: 03212 7838.

Glasgow Museum of Transport, Kelvin Hall, 1 Bunhouse Road, Glasgow G3 8PZ. Telephone: 041-357 3929.

Grampian Transport Museum, Alford, Aberdeenshire AB3 8AD. Telephone: 09755 62292.

Haynes Sparkford Motor Museum, Sparkford, Yeovil, Somerset BA22 7LH. Telephone: 0963 40804.

Heritage Motor Museum (British Motor Industry Heritage Trust), Syon Park, Brentford, Middlesex TW8 3JF. Telephone: 081-560 1378.

Jersey Motor Museum, St Peter's Village, Jersey, Channel Islands. Telephone: 0534 82966.

Manx Motor Museum, Crosby, Isle of Man. Telephone: 0624 851236.

Museum of British Road Transport, St Agnes Lane, Hales Street, Coventry, West Midlands CV1 1PN. Telephone: 0203 832425.

Myreton Motor Museum, Aberlady, East Lothian EH32 0PZ. Telephone: 08757 288.

National Motor Museum, John Montagu Building, Beaulieu, Hampshire SO42 7ZN. Telephone: 0590 612345.

National Museum of Irish Transport, Scotts Garden, Killarney, County Kerry, Republic of Ireland. Telephone: 010-353-64 32638.

Peter Black Collection, Lawkholme Lane, Keighley, West Yorkshire BD21 3JQ. Telephone: 0535 661177.

Royal Museum of Scotland, Chambers Street, Edinburgh EH1 1JF. Telephone: 031-225 7534.

Sandringham Museum, Sandringham House, King's Lynn, Norfolk PE35 6EN. Telephone: 0553 772675. Royal cars.

Science Museum, Exhibition Road, South Kensington, London SW7 2DD. Telephone: 071-938 8000.

The Shuttleworth Collection, Old Warden Aerodrome, Biggleswade, Bedfordshire SG18 9ER. Telephone: 076727 288.

Streetlife — Hull Museum of Transport, High Street, Hull, North Humberside. Telephone: 0482 222737 or 222738.

Ulster Folk and Transport Museum, Cultra, Holywood, County Down, Northern Ireland BT18 0EU. Telephone: 0232 428428.